Genre Realistic

Essential Questi

How are families around the world the same and different?

by Parker Wu

illustrated by Akemi Gutierrez

Chapter 1
The Best Time of the Year!

My name is Max. I am getting ready for the Chinese New Year. I will celebrate it with my family.

"This is the best time of the year!" says my brother Lee.

"I've been looking forward to this," I say.

Lee is older than I am. He's
fourteen. Mostly, we get along. Lee
hasn't been here much this week.

"He's very busy," says Granddad.

Granddad grew up in China. His first
language is Mandarin. He's teaching
me to speak it. I love to hear
Granddad tell stories.

Our family is busy this week! Aunt Lin and Mom made a list of things to do. First, we must clean the house.

"We have to sweep away the old year," says Mom. "Then we can start the new one."

1. Clean the house.
2. Plan the feast.
3. Go shopping.
4. Cook the feast.

I share a bedroom with Lee. "Our room is already clean," I tell Mom.

"It is clean," she says. "But it must be spotless for the New Year."

"Lee should help," I say.

But Lee is not at home.

"He's got other things to do today," said Mom. "He has to practice."

"For what?" I asked.

"You'll see," said Mom. So I cleaned our room by myself, which didn't seem fair.

Chapter 2
Getting Ready for the Feast

We have been cooking all week. Yesterday, I helped Aunt Lin make some taro cakes and other sweets.

"You can help us today too," Mom says. She knows I love cooking.

We go to the market to buy more food. I help my mother and aunt shop for meat and vegetables.

At home, Mom says, "It's time to make dumplings." That will be fun!

"I love making dumplings," I say.

Then Lee comes home. He has been gone all day.

"Tell me where you've been," I plead. But Lee just smiles. He says that will be a surprise.

Chapter 3
The New Year's Feast

In the evening, we hear the doorbell. "Here they are," says Aunt Lin.

It's our cousins. We have invited them for the feast. It's time to eat!

Everything looks so good. My favorites are the dumplings and the fish. Lee likes the duck. Everyone says it is the best meal ever.

After the feast, Granddad takes us aside. He gives us each a New Year's present. It's a red envelope with coins inside. Then Granddad winks at Lee. "Good luck for tomorrow," he says.

Then, we all say good night. Tomorrow we will watch the parade with music, dancing, and a big dragon!

Chapter 4
The Dragon's Feet

The next day, our neighbor, Mr. Jing, arrives early. Lee opens the door. "Are you ready, Lee?" Mr. Jing says.

"Where are you going?" I ask.

But Lee just says, "See you later."

The rest of our family goes to see the parade. It's starting, but I don't see Lee. I hope he doesn't miss it.

Here comes the dragon! I like watching the dragon. It is the star of the parade. Its long body goes all the way down the block. Everyone scurries out of its way.

Wait—I think I know those shoes! So that's where Lee has been. He must have been practicing for the parade!

We meet Lee after the parade.

"Did you see me?" he asks.

"Yes!" I say. "Your feet made great dragon's feet!" Everyone laughs.

"Happy New Year!" I say to Lee.

Respond to Reading

Summarize

Use important details to help you summarize *Happy New Year!*

Character	Setting	Events

Text Evidence

1. How do you know that *Happy New Year!* is realistic fiction? Genre

2. Why does Max think this time of year is special and important? Use story details to support your answer. Character, Setting, Events

3. Use what you know about root words to figure out the meaning of *cooking* on page 7. Root Words

4. Write about things that tell you what Max is like. Write About Reading

Compare Texts
Read how families in different countries celebrate the new year.

New Year's Eve

Cultures around the world mark the new year in many ways. In Spain, people share something sweet. At midnight on New Year's Eve, they eat twelve grapes. People hope that eating them will bring them twelve sweet months of the year.

On New Year's Eve in Scotland, everyone sings together at midnight. The first person to enter after midnight brings a small gift. It could be a piece of bread or coal. If they do, the tradition says the house will have food and heat all year.

In Ecuador, people make scarecrows. They often decorate them with masks. Then they write down things they have done wrong. They tie the list to the scarecrow. At midnight, they set it on fire. Their old mistakes burn up. Now they can begin the year with a fresh start.

Make Connections

What are some ways people celebrate the new year? Essential Question

Compare Max's new year with another new year tradition you read about.

Text to Text

Focus on
Social Studies

Purpose To compare ways we celebrate special occasions

What to Do

Step 1 Tell a partner about how your family celebrates a special occasion. It could be a holiday or birthday.

Step 2 Draw a picture that shows the special things you see or do.

Step 3 Add labels to your picture. Label the special things you see or do.

Step 4 Share your picture with your partner. Are the things you do alike or different?